U.S.A. TRAVEL GUIDES

NEBRASKA

BY ANN HEINRICHS • ILLUSTRATED BY MATT KANIA

The Child's World®
childsworld.com

Published by The Child's World®
1980 Lookout Drive • Mankato, MN 56003-1705
800-599-READ • www.childsworld.com

ISBN 9781503819672
LCCN 2016961180

Printing
Printed in the United States of America
PA02334

Ann Heinrichs is the author
of more than 100 books
for children and young
adults. She has also enjoyed
successful careers as a
children's book editor and
an advertising copywriter.
Ann grew up in Fort Smith,
Arkansas, and lives in
Chicago, Illinois.

About the Author
Ann Heinrichs

Matt Kania loves maps and, as a
kid, dreamed of making them. In
school he studied geography and
cartography, and today he makes
maps for a living. Matt's favorite
thing about drawing maps is
learning about the places they
represent. Many of the maps
he has created can be found in
books, magazines, videos, Web
sites, and public places.

About the
Map Illustrator
Matt Kania

*On the cover: Chimney Rock was a landmark for people
traveling through Nebraska on the Oregon Trail.*

OUR NEBRASKA TRIP

NEBRASKA

Ready for a trip through Nebraska? You're in for quite a ride! You'll hang out with fur traders and cowboys. You'll watch dancing birds and trick dogs. You'll feed fish and cluck like a chicken. You'll see golden wheat fields and grazing cattle. And you'll see skeletons millions of years old. Not bad for one state!

Just follow that dotted line or skip around. Either way, you're in for an exciting tour. Are you all buckled up? Then we're on our way!

WELCOME TO
NEBRASKA

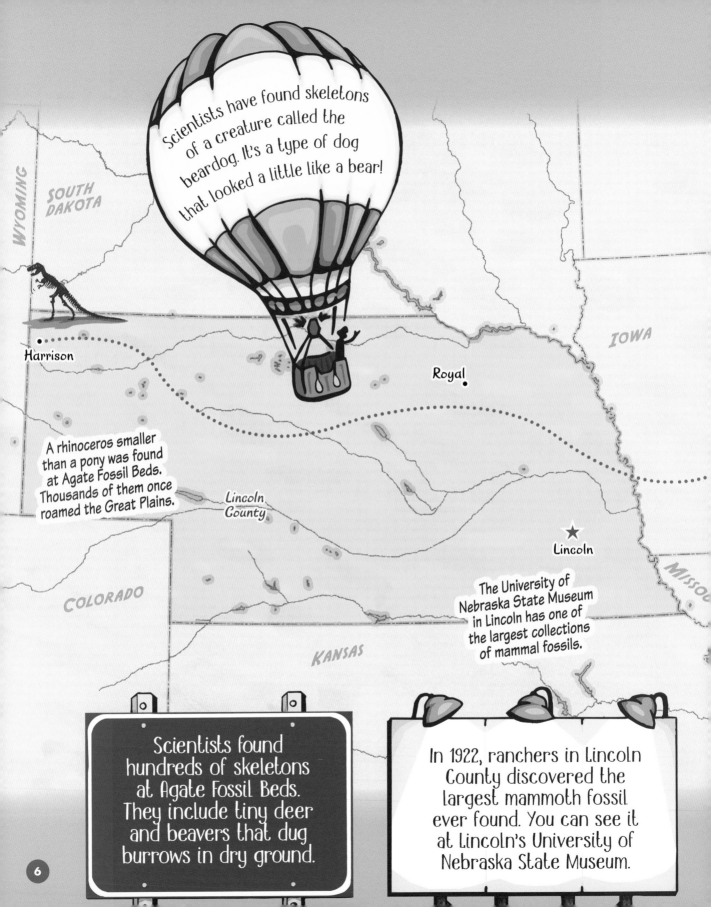

Scientists have found skeletons of a creature called the beardog. It's a type of dog that looked a little like a bear!

WYOMING

SOUTH DAKOTA

Harrison

IOWA

Royal

A rhinoceros smaller than a pony was found at Agate Fossil Beds. Thousands of them once roamed the Great Plains.

Lincoln County

★ Lincoln

COLORADO

The University of Nebraska State Museum in Lincoln has one of the largest collections of mammal fossils.

KANSAS

MISSOU

Scientists found hundreds of skeletons at Agate Fossil Beds. They include tiny deer and beavers that dug burrows in dry ground.

In 1922, ranchers in Lincoln County discovered the largest mammoth fossil ever found. You can see it at Lincoln's University of Nebraska State Museum.

Yikes! Look at the big pointy teeth on that hog!

AGATE FOSSIL BEDS

Scary skeletons are everywhere! Watch out for that *Dinohyus*. Its name means "terrible pig." And steer clear of that *Moropus*. This enormous horse could stand on its hind legs.

You're at Agate **Fossil** Beds. It's in far-western Nebraska, near Harrison. The skeletons are in the visitors' center. Scientists dug them up from the surrounding area.

The animals are about 20 million years old. What happened to them? Scientists believe Nebraska was having a **drought**. Thirsty animals gathered at a water hole here. Slowly it dried up, and they died.

Ashfall Fossil Beds State Historical Park is in Royal.

Dinohyus lived in the Miocene Era, 5.3 million years ago.

Scotts Bluff was named after Hiram Scott. He was a fur trapper. He died near the bluff in 1828.

Imagine you're a **pioneer** headed west. You would know you had arrived at Scotts Bluff National Monument. These rocky cliffs rise high over the plains. You might have seen Chimney Rock, near Bayard. These tall rock formations rise in western Nebraska.

Rolling plains cover most of Nebraska. They make rich farmland and grazing land. The Sand Hills are in north-central Nebraska. Here, wind has blown the sandy soil into piles.

The Platte River is Nebraska's major river. It begins where two rivers join. They are the North Platte and the South Platte. The Platte River flows into the Missouri River. The Missouri River forms Nebraska's eastern border.

Learn about covered wagons at Scotts Bluff.

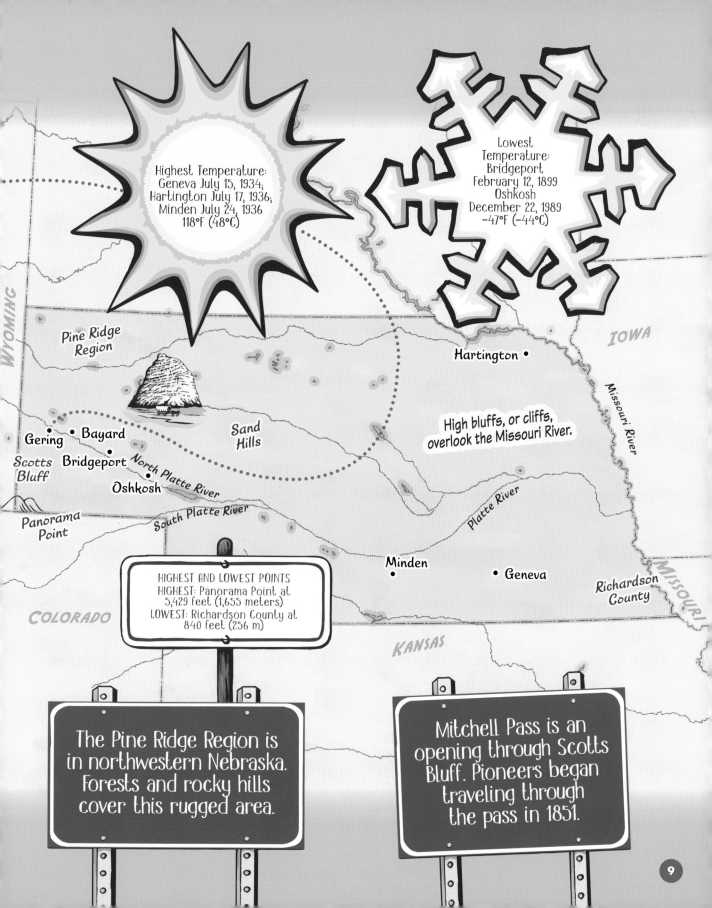

Highest Temperature:
Geneva July 15, 1934;
Hartington July 17, 1936;
Minden July 24, 1936
118°F (48°C)

Lowest
Temperature:
Bridgeport
February 12, 1899
Oshkosh
December 22, 1989
–47°F (–44°C)

WYOMING

Pine Ridge
Region

IOWA

Hartington •

High bluffs, or cliffs,
overlook the Missouri River.

Missouri River

Gering • Bayard
Scotts
Bluff
Bridgeport
Oshkosh

Sand
Hills

North Platte River

Panorama
Point

South Platte River

Platte River

Minden •

• Geneva

Richardson
County

COLORADO

HIGHEST AND LOWEST POINTS
HIGHEST: Panorama Point at
5,429 feet (1,655 meters)
LOWEST: Richardson County at
840 feet (256 m)

KANSAS

MISSOURI

The Pine Ridge Region is
in northwestern Nebraska.
Forests and rocky hills
cover this rugged area.

Mitchell Pass is an
opening through Scotts
Bluff. Pioneers began
traveling through
the pass in 1851.

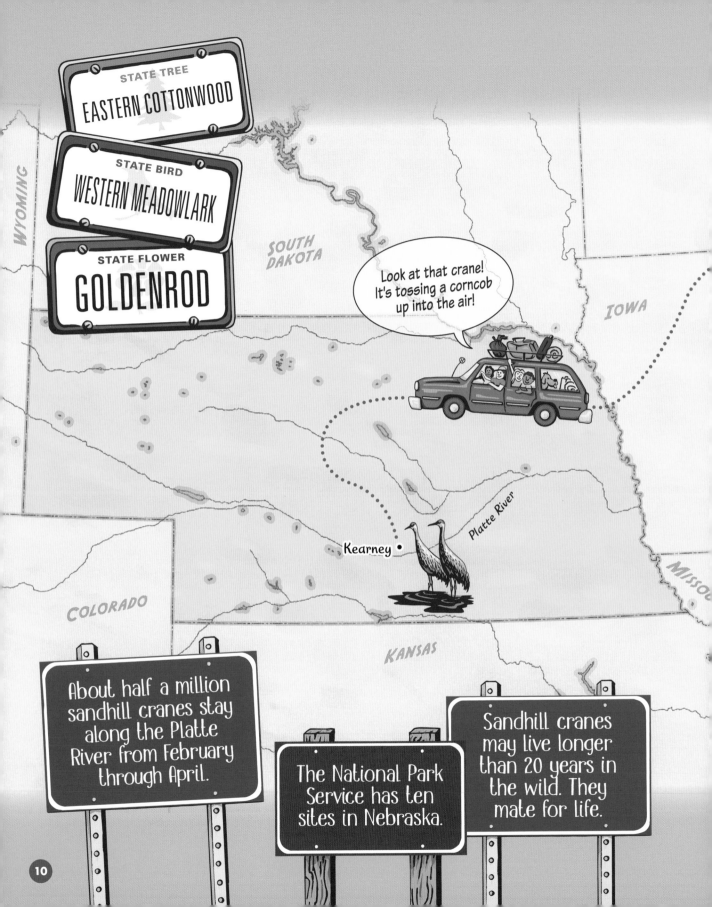

STATE TREE
EASTERN COTTONWOOD

STATE BIRD
WESTERN MEADOWLARK

STATE FLOWER
GOLDENROD

WYOMING

SOUTH DAKOTA

IOWA

Look at that crane! It's tossing a corncob up into the air!

Platte River

MISSOURI

Kearney

COLORADO

KANSAS

About half a million sandhill cranes stay along the Platte River from February through April.

The National Park Service has ten sites in Nebraska.

Sandhill cranes may live longer than 20 years in the wild. They mate for life.

The long-legged birds stretch out their wings. They gracefully bow down to each other. Then they spring high into the air!

You're watching the dance of the sandhill cranes. These awesome birds gather along the Platte River. Many of them can be seen east of Kearney. They feed in the cornfields. They dance to attract a mate.

Many other animals live in Nebraska all year. They include deer, prairie dogs, badgers, and coyotes.

Nebraska doesn't have much forestland. Prairies once covered much of the state. Prairies are grasslands where tall grasses grow. But farmers plowed up much of these grasslands to grow crops.

Sandhill cranes dance throughout the year, though it is most frequent during mating season.

THE WAYNE CHICKEN SHOW

Would you like to enter the National Cluck-Off? You don't have to do much. Just act and sound like a chicken. And keep it up for 15 seconds!

It all happens at the Wayne Chicken Show. This festival celebrates a favorite Nebraska farm animal.

Nebraska is one of the top farming states. Fields of wheat stretch across the western plains. The north-central region is good for grazing cattle. Farmers in the east grow many different crops, including popcorn.

Beef cattle are Nebraska's most valuable farm animals. Hogs are important, too. Farmers sell their meat all over the country. Corn is the state's leading crop. Farmers also raise wheat, soybeans, and hay.

Avoca holds the Quack-Off Duck Race every year.

Chickens are everywhere at the Wayne Chicken Show!

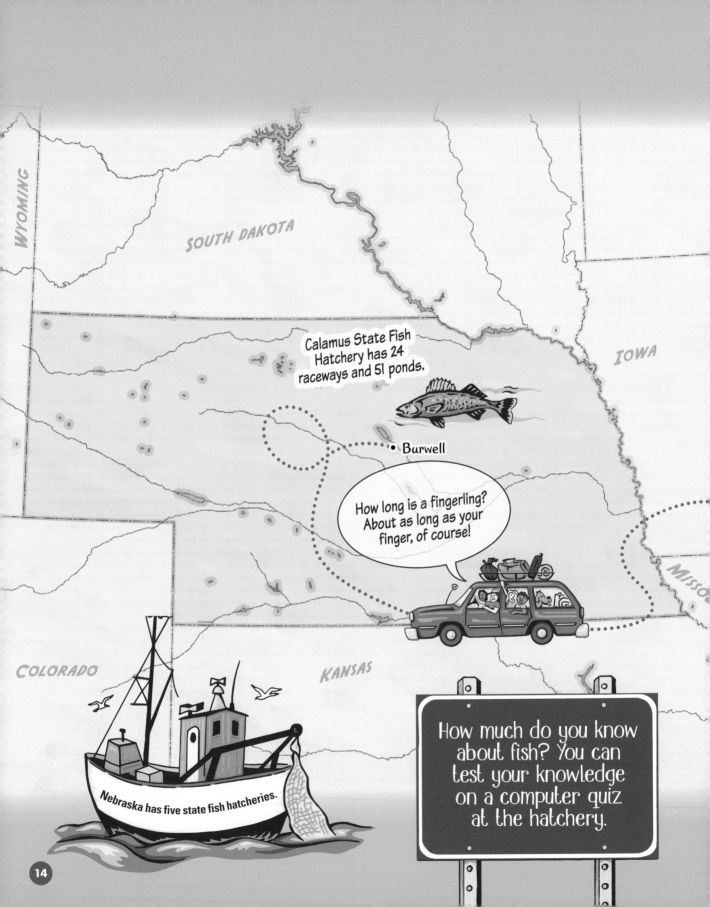

CALAMUS STATE FISH HATCHERY IN BURWELL

Where do fish live? In rivers, lakes, and oceans, of course! But those aren't the only fish homes. Some fish come from hatcheries. Hatcheries are like big fish farms!

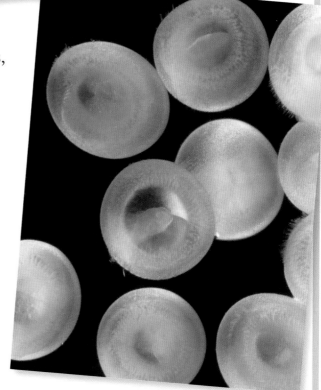

Just visit Calamus State Fish Hatchery in Burwell. It grows catfish, walleye, trout, and other fish. Workers watch over thousands of fish eggs. Small fish, called fry, hatch from the eggs. When they're a little bigger, they're called fingerlings.

The hatchery releases fry and fingerlings into streams and lakes, where the fish grow up. If you catch a fish in Nebraska, it may have come from the hatchery!

The fish at Calamus State Fish Hatchery start out as eggs.

THE WINNEBAGO POWWOW

The dancers wear colorful feathers and beads. Fringe and feathers swirl around as they dance. This is the Winnebago Powwow. The Winnebago people hold this festival every year near Winnebago. They perform many **traditional** dances.

Many Native American groups live in Nebraska. In the past, some hunted bison across the plains. They lived in teepees made of animal skins. Others lived in earth lodges. They hunted and grew corn and other vegetables.

French explorers crossed Nebraska in 1739. Soon, French fur trappers and traders arrived. They traded with Native Americans for furs. In 1803, the United States purchased from France the land that would become Nebraska.

The powwow takes place in Winnebago to honor the Winnebago's last war chief, Little Priest.

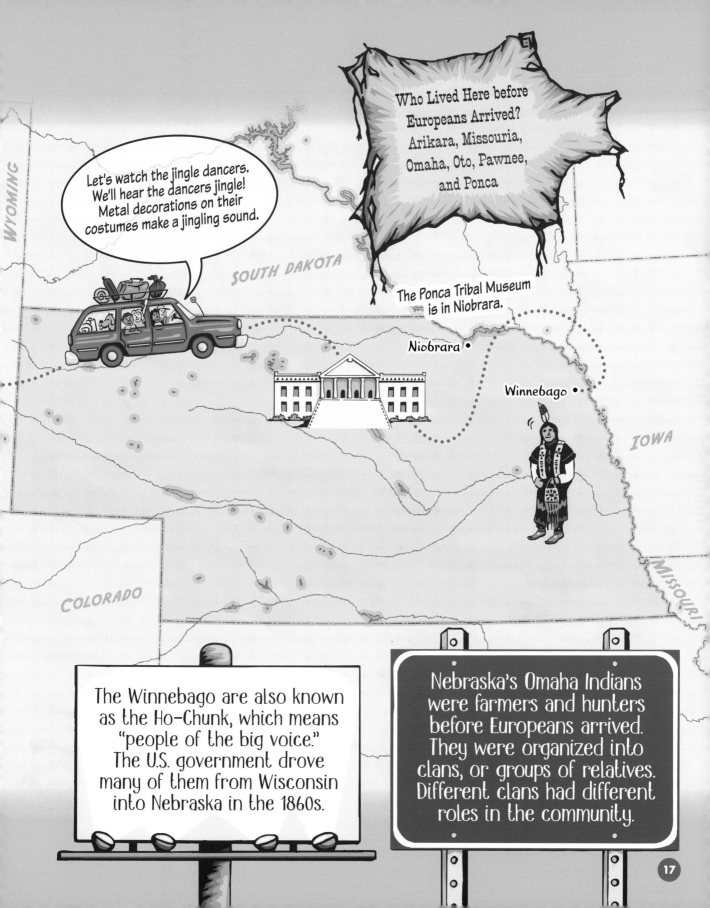

Who Lived Here before Europeans Arrived? Arikara, Missouria, Omaha, Oto, Pawnee, and Ponca

Let's watch the jingle dancers. We'll hear the dancers jingle! Metal decorations on their costumes make a jingling sound.

The Ponca Tribal Museum is in Niobrara.

Niobrara •

Winnebago •

WYOMING

SOUTH DAKOTA

IOWA

MISSOURI

COLORADO

The Winnebago are also known as the Ho-Chunk, which means "people of the big voice." The U.S. government drove many of them from Wisconsin into Nebraska in the 1860s.

Nebraska's Omaha Indians were farmers and hunters before Europeans arrived. They were organized into clans, or groups of relatives. Different clans had different roles in the community.

The U.S. Congress established Nebraska Territory in 1854. This opened the region to settlement.

Look! It's the flag ceremony! Kids and grown-ups are marching along with flags. They're flags of the nations that were involved in the fur trade.

The Museum of the Fur Trade is near Chadron. It displays many objects from the fur-trade days.

In 1820, Nebraska's first library was established at the Fort Atkinson military post.

Chadron was the site of a trading post. It operated from 1837 to 1876.

The Oregon Trail ran from Independence, Missouri, to Oregon, on the west coast.

Fort Lisa was just north of Omaha. Manuel Lisa opened it in 1814. There he sold or traded blankets, food, guns, and other goods.

FUR TRADE DAYS IN CHADRON

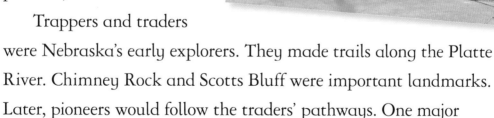

Put on your **buckskins**. It's time for Fur Trade Days! Chadron holds this festival every year. People dress like 1800s fur traders. They put up tents just like fur traders did. They enjoy shooting demonstrations, music, parades, and fireworks.

Trappers and traders were Nebraska's early explorers. They made trails along the Platte River. Chimney Rock and Scotts Bluff were important landmarks. Later, pioneers would follow the traders' pathways. One major route became the Oregon Trail.

Fur companies began setting up trading posts. Bellevue began as a fur-trading post in 1823. It was Nebraska's first permanent settlement.

Chadron was established as a fur-trading post in 1841.

GOTHENBURG'S SOD HOUSE MUSEUM

Plants are growing on the roof. The walls are built of **sod**. Inside, the floors are powdery dirt. This is a sod house. It's part of Gothenburg's Sod House Museum.

Early settlers in Nebraska built sod homes. They found few trees for building houses. Many settlers had come over the Oregon Trail. They hauled all they owned in covered wagons. The wagon wheels left deep ruts, or grooves. You can still see those wheel ruts today.

In 1862, the U.S. government passed the Homestead Act. It offered free or cheap land to settlers if they worked it for five years. Then thousands of pioneers poured into Nebraska.

Pioneers took the Oregon, California, and Mormon trails through Nebraska.

Sod houses were built with bricks made of dirt.

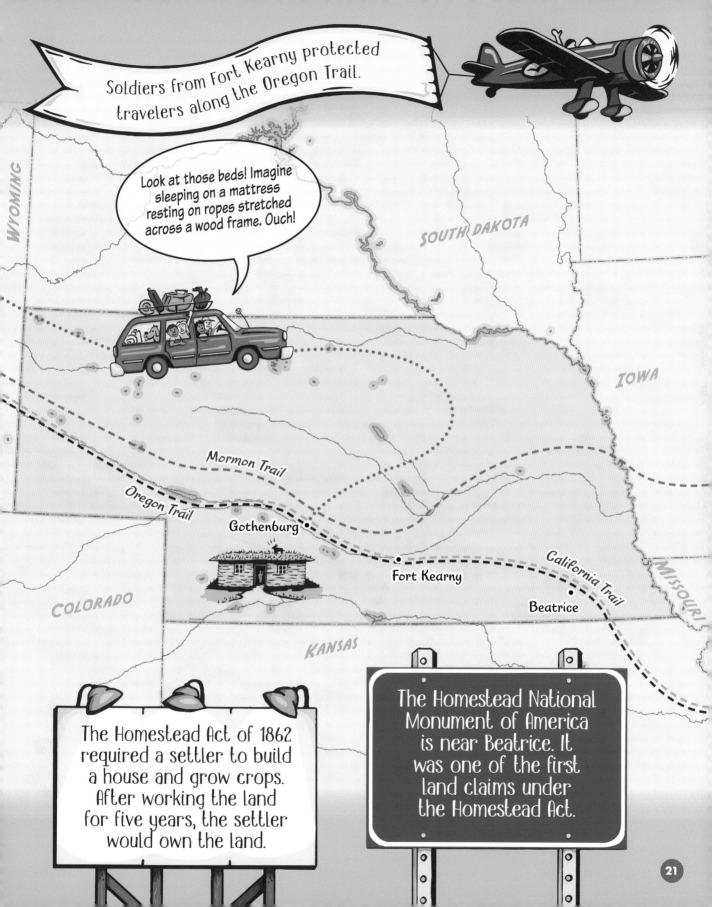

In 2016, 1,907,116 people lived in Nebraska. It's the 37th-largest state by population.

Yum! Let's make a beeline for the aebleskiver—Danish pancakes!

Before 1960, most Nebraskans lived in rural areas. Those are areas outside of cities and towns. By 2013, almost two out of three Nebraskans lived in cities or towns.

WYOMING

SOUTH DAKOTA

COLORADO

KANSAS

IOWA

Omaha
Bellevue
Syracuse
Lincoln
Wilber
Dannebrog
Platte River
Missouri River
MISSO...

POPULATION OF LARGEST CITIES
Omaha.........................443,885
Lincoln........................277,348
Bellevue........................55,510

Grundlovsfest is also called Danish Day. It honors the signing of Denmark's constitution, or basic set of laws, in 1849.

Nebraskans aren't spread evenly across the state. Most people live along the Missouri and Platte rivers.

GRUNDLOVSFEST IN DANNEBROG

Take a pony ride. Gobble up some Danish pastries. Then watch the costumed dancers whirl around. You're enjoying Grundlovsfest in Dannebrog!

This festival celebrates the town's Danish **heritage**. (The word Danish means things related to Denmark.)

Immigrants from many lands settled in Nebraska. Many towns still celebrate their settlers' heritage. For example, Wilber holds a Czech Days festival. Syracuse holds a GermanFest. One event is the Viener Dog Races. It's a race for dachshunds. They're often called wiener dogs. Why? Because their bodies are long—like hot dogs, which are also called wiener dogs!

Enjoy some aebleskiver *at Grundlovsfest!*

STUHR MUSEUM IN GRAND ISLAND

Meet the blacksmith and the tinsmith. Stop by the hatmaker's shop. Or just drop into someone's home. You're visiting Stuhr Museum of the Prairie Pioneer. It's built like a Nebraska prairie community. Many towns like this sprang up along train routes.

Workers first built railroads across Nebraska in 1865. Then pioneers began arriving by train. Some opened shops in the new towns. Others plowed and planted crops. Grasshoppers swarmed across the land in the 1870s. They destroyed acres of crops. Many farmers left the state.

The church at the Stuhr Museum was built in 1888.

Nebraska was the 37th state to enter the Union. It joined on March 1, 1867.

Hey, watch that tinsmith! He has cookie cutters in the shape of each of the 50 states!

The Union Pacific Railroad was completed across Nebraska in 1867. It followed the Platte River for much of its route.

The Union Pacific Railroad was part of the transcontinental railroad. This train line crossed the entire United States. It was completed in 1869.

The Union Station Gallery is at Omaha's Durham Museum. It was one of the Union Pacific's train stations in Omaha.

Hey, Dad! They've got a cake-baking event. You can try out your Mystery Mix or your Disaster Delight!

WYOMING

SOUTH DAKOTA

IOWA

Pine Ridge Region

Niobrara River

Laurel •

The Buffalo Bill Rodeo is named for William Cody. He was known as Buffalo Bill. His ranch is in North Platte.

• North Platte

Omaha •

Grand Island •

Platte River

• Hastings

MISSOU

• Filley

COLORADO

KANSAS

ACTORS BORN IN NEBRASKA
Fred Astaire (Omaha)
Marlon Brando (Omaha)
Montgomery Clift (Omaha)
James Coburn (Laurel)

Sandy Dennis (Hastings)
Henry Fonda (Grand Island)
Dorothy McGuire (Omaha)
Nick Nolte (Omaha)
Robert Taylor (Filley)

Buffalo Bill Cody held his Old Glory Blowout in North Platte in 1882. It is said to be the first rodeo. Bill toured the country with his Wild West shows.

Cowboys cling for their life to bucking **broncos**. Other cowboys are riding bulls or roping calves. You're watching the Buffalo Bill Rodeo! It's part of North Platte's Nebraskaland Days celebration. Besides the rodeo, there are parades, rodeos, and barbecues.

You can have lots of fun in Nebraska. Most counties have fairs in the summer. Thousands of people attend Grand Island's Nebraska State Fair.

Campers and hikers enjoy the Pine Ridge Region. This forested area is in western Nebraska. Many people head for the Platte or Niobrara rivers. They go fishing or just enjoy nature.

Meet some horses at Nebraskaland Days.

OFFUTT AIR FORCE BASE NEAR BELLEVUE

Look out from the aircraft control tower. Chat with firefighters in the fire department. Visit the weather station. Then watch a military dog follow commands.

You're touring Offutt Air Force Base near Bellevue. It's home to the U.S. Strategic Command. This center controls the nation's **nuclear** forces.

Nebraska developed many new **industries** in the 1900s. Many insurance companies made Nebraska their **headquarters**, too. Oil became an important industry in southeast Nebraska. And factories opened throughout the state.

Offutt Air Force Base holds training exercises to prepare for possible attacks against the United States.

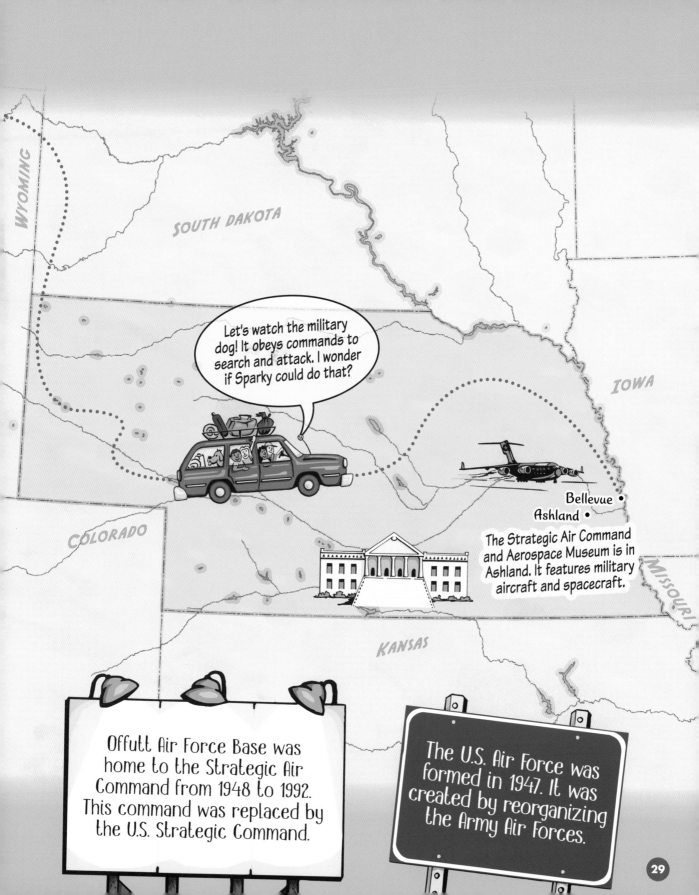

Let's watch the military dog! It obeys commands to search and attack. I wonder if Sparky could do that?

Bellevue •
Ashland •

The Strategic Air Command and Aerospace Museum is in Ashland. It features military aircraft and spacecraft.

Offutt Air Force Base was home to the Strategic Air Command from 1948 to 1992. This command was replaced by the U.S. Strategic Command.

The U.S. Air Force was formed in 1947. It was created by reorganizing the Army Air Forces.

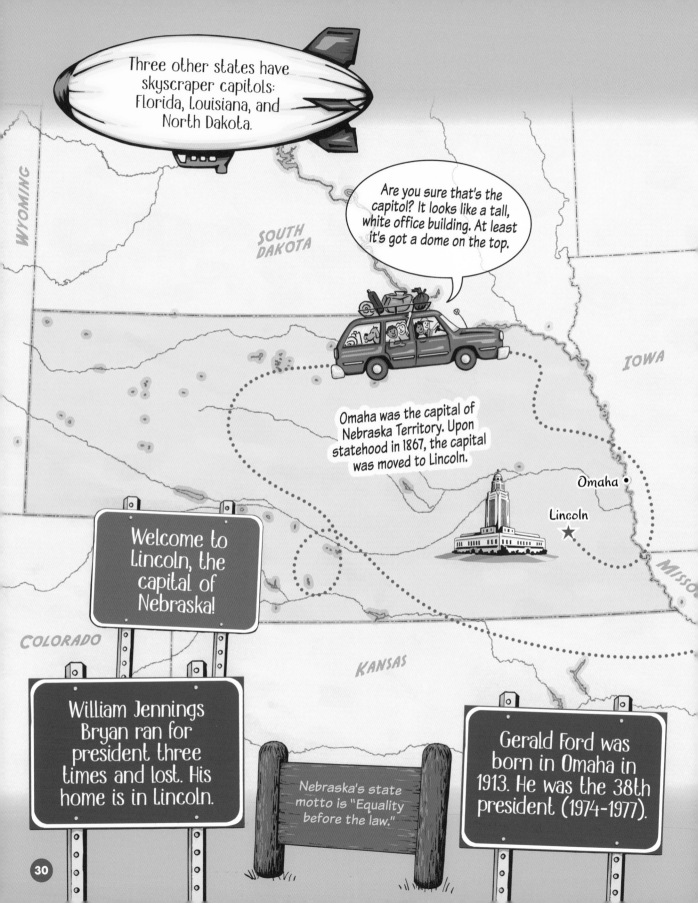

THE STATE CAPITOL IN LINCOLN

Most state capitols are just a few stories high. But Nebraska's capitol is a **skyscraper**. Its office tower is 15 stories high.

Inside are many state government offices. Nebraska has three branches of government. One branch makes the state's laws. It's called the state legislature. Nebraska's legislature is unusual, just like its capitol. All the other states have a two-house legislature. But not Nebraska. Its legislature has only one house.

The governor heads another branch of government. It carries out the laws. Courts make up the third branch. They decide whether someone has broken the law.

The outside walls of the capitol are covered in limestone.

P ut on your safety glasses! You're touring Kawasaki Motors Manufacturing in Lincoln! The factory is more than 1,600 feet (488 m) long. You'll see workers putting the finishing touches on ATVs. You'll see robots welding and painting. They also make trains!

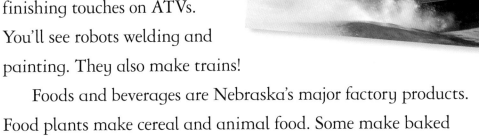

Foods and beverages are Nebraska's major factory products. Food plants make cereal and animal food. Some make baked goods or dairy products.

Meatpacking is a huge Nebraska industry. Meatpacking plants cut and package beef and pork.

Chemicals are another important factory product. They include medicines, bug killers, and fertilizer. Many Nebraska factories make farm machines, too.

Boaters enjoy racing across the water on Kawasaki Jet Skis.

What's Made in Nebraska? Food products, chemicals, and machinery

Look! That small tow truck is actually a robot named Mad Max. He plays a song as he collects empty carts from the production line.

Joyce C. Hall was born in David City. He founded the Hallmark greeting card company.

WYOMING

SOUTH DAKOTA

IOWA

• Sidney

David City •

Lincoln ★

MISSOURI

Cabela's sells hunting and outdoor gear. It is based in Sidney.

KANSAS

COLORADO

Kawasaki Motors Manufacturing in Lincoln makes many vehicles including ATVs, utility vehicles, and personal watercraft.

What's Mined in Nebraska? Petroleum, sand, and gravel

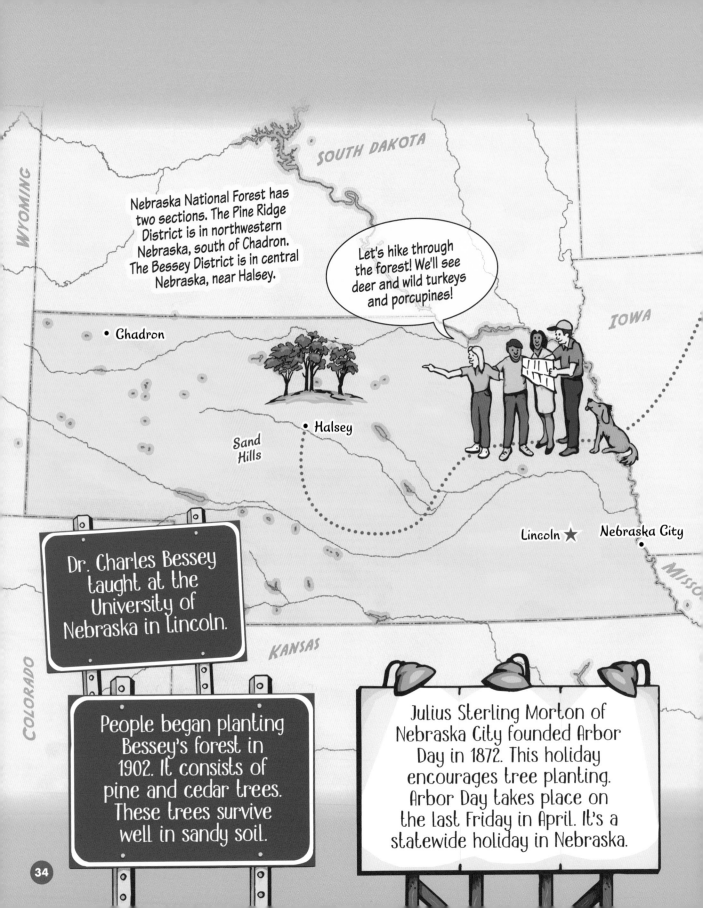

Nebraska National Forest has two sections. The Pine Ridge District is in northwestern Nebraska, south of Chadron. The Bessey District is in central Nebraska, near Halsey.

Let's hike through the forest! We'll see deer and wild turkeys and porcupines!

WYOMING

SOUTH DAKOTA

IOWA

• Chadron

Sand Hills

• Halsey

Lincoln ★   Nebraska City

MISSO

KANSAS

COLORADO

Dr. Charles Bessey taught at the University of Nebraska in Lincoln.

People began planting Bessey's forest in 1902. It consists of pine and cedar trees. These trees survive well in sandy soil.

Julius Sterling Morton of Nebraska City founded Arbor Day in 1872. This holiday encourages tree planting. Arbor Day takes place on the last Friday in April. It's a statewide holiday in Nebraska.

THE HAND-PLANTED FOREST NEAR HALSEY

Have you ever planted a tree? It's not that easy to do. Just imagine planting a whole forest of trees! That's what Dr. Charles Bessey decided to do. He was a botanist, or plant scientist. He knew Nebraska's plains had few trees. He believed trees could grow in the sandy soil. So he decided to grow some.

Bessey's helpers planted thousands of trees. Those trees became the world's largest hand-planted forest. They were like a green island in the Sand Hills. They're now in Nebraska National Forest, near Halsey. Just climb up Scott Lookout Tower. You can look out over Bessey's dream!

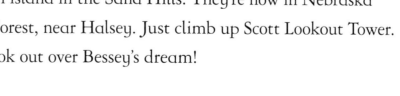

Some people ride horses through Nebraska National Forest.

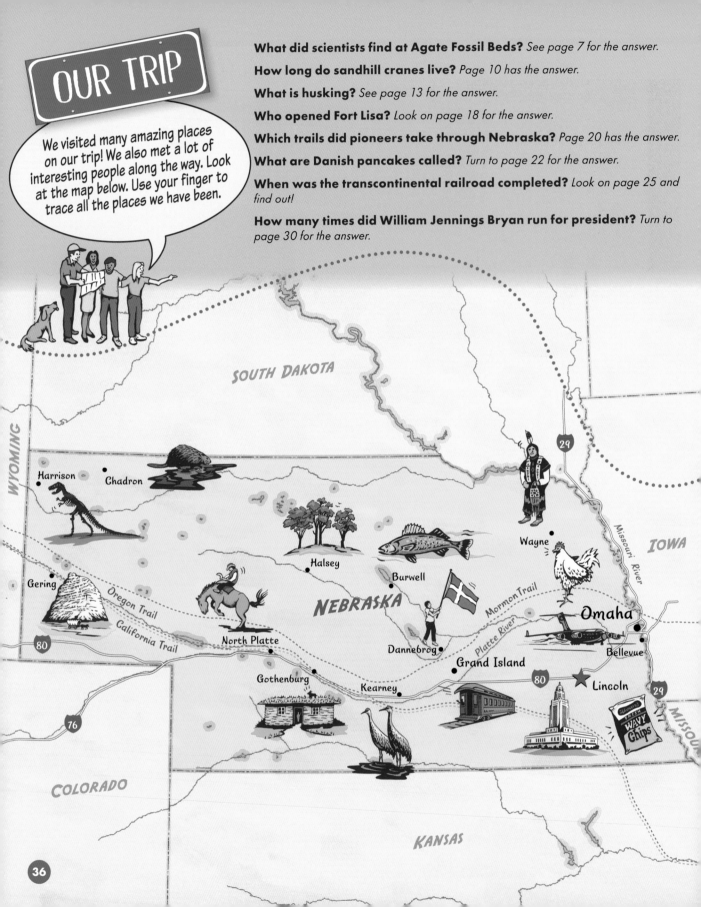

OUR TRIP

We visited many amazing places on our trip! We also met a lot of interesting people along the way. Look at the map below. Use your finger to trace all the places we have been.

What did scientists find at Agate Fossil Beds? *See page 7 for the answer.*

How long do sandhill cranes live? *Page 10 has the answer.*

What is husking? *See page 13 for the answer.*

Who opened Fort Lisa? *Look on page 18 for the answer.*

Which trails did pioneers take through Nebraska? *Page 20 has the answer.*

What are Danish pancakes called? *Turn to page 22 for the answer.*

When was the transcontinental railroad completed? *Look on page 25 and find out!*

How many times did William Jennings Bryan run for president? *Turn to page 30 for the answer.*

SOUTH DAKOTA

WYOMING

Harrison · Chadron

Halsey

Burwell

NEBRASKA

Wayne

IOWA

Gering

Oregon Trail

California Trail

North Platte

Dannebrog

Mormon Trail

Platte River

Omaha

Bellevue

Grand Island

Gothenburg

Kearney

80

Lincoln

29

MISSOURI

Missouri River

76

COLORADO

KANSAS

State flag

State seal

That was a great trip! We have traveled all over Nebraska! There are a few places that we didn't have time for, though. Next time, we plan to visit the Heartland of America Park and Fountain in Omaha. This park is located along the Missouri River and features a lake, fountains, a waterfall, and a walking path.

STATE SYMBOLS

State beverage: Milk

State bird: Western meadowlark

State fish: Channel catfish

State flower: Goldenrod

State folk dance: Square dance

State fossil: Mammoth

State gem: Blue chalcedony (blue agate)

State grass: Little bluestem

State insect: Honeybee

State mammal: White-tailed deer

State river: Platte River

State rock: Prairie agate

State soft drink: Kool-Aid

State soil: Holdrege series

State tree: Eastern cottonwood

STATE SONG

"BEAUTIFUL NEBRASKA"
Words by Jim Fras and Guy G. Miller,
Music by Jim Fras

Beautiful Nebraska, peaceful prairieland,
Laced with many rivers, and the hills
   of sand;
Dark green valleys cradled in the earth,
Rain and sunshine bring abundant birth.

Beautiful Nebraska, as you look around,
You will find a rainbow reaching to
   the ground;
All these wonders by the Master's hand;
Beautiful Nebraska land.

We are so proud of this state where we live,
There is no place that has so much to give.

Beautiful Nebraska, as you look around,
You will find a rainbow reaching to the
   ground;
All these wonders by the Master's hand,
Beautiful Nebraska land.

FAMOUS PEOPLE

Abbott, Grace (1878–1939), social worker

Astaire, Fred (1899–1987), dancer and actor

Brando, Marlon (1924–2004), actor

Buffett, Warren (1930–), philanthropist and businessman

Carson, Johnny (1925–2005), entertainer

Cather, Willa (1873–1947), author

Chamberlain, Joba (1985–), baseball player

Cheney, Richard (1941–), vice president to George W. Bush

Cruikshank, Lucas (1993–), YouTube star

Fonda, Henry (1905–1982), actor

Ford, Gerald (1913–2006), 38th U.S. president

Gordon, Alex (1984–), baseball player

Helgenberger, Marg (1958–), actor

La Flesche, Susette (1854–1903), Omaha Native American rights activist and author

Lawhead, Stephen R. (1950–), author

Malcolm X (1925–1965), civil rights leader

Nolte, Nick (1941–), actor

Red Cloud (1822–1909), Oglala Lakota chief

Sparks, Nicholas (1965–), author

Standing Bear (ca. 1834–1908), Ponca chief

WORDS TO KNOW

broncos (BRONG-koz) wild or untrained horses

buckskins (BUHK-skinz) clothes made from the skin of a deer

drought (DROUT) a lack of rain

fossil (FOSS-uhl) a print or the remains of a plant or animal that lived long ago

headquarters (HED-kwor-turz) an organization's main office location

heritage (HER-uh-tij) customs passed down from earlier times

immigrants (IM-uh-gruhnts) people who leave their home country and settle in a new land

industries (IN-duh-streez) types of businesses

nuclear (NOO-klee-ur) producing energy from the splitting of tiny particles called atoms

pioneer (pye-uh-NEER) a person who moves into an unsettled land

skyscraper (SKYE-skray-pur) a very tall building

sod (SOD) chunks of earth with grass and roots attached

traditional (truh-DISH-uhn-ul) passed down from one generation to another

TO LEARN MORE

IN THE LIBRARY

Coleman, Miriam. *Nebraska: The Cornhusker State*. New York, NY: PowerKids Press, 2011.

Perish, Patrick. *Nebraska: The Cornhusker State*. Minneapolis, MN: Bellwether Media, 2014.

Sanders, Doug, and Pete Schauer. *Nebraska*. New York, NY: Cavendish Square, 2017.

ON THE WEB
Visit our Web site for links about Nebraska:
childsworld.com/links

*Note to Parents, Teachers, and Librarians: We routinely verify our Web links to make sure
they are safe and active sites. So encourage your readers to check them out!*

PLACES TO VISIT OR CONTACT
Nebraska State Historical Society
nebraskahistory.org
PO Box 82554
Lincoln, NE 68501-2554
402/471-3270
For more information about the history of Nebraska

Nebraska Tourism Commission
visitnebraska.com
PO Box 98907
Lincoln, NE 68509-8907
402/471-3796
For more information about traveling in Nebraska

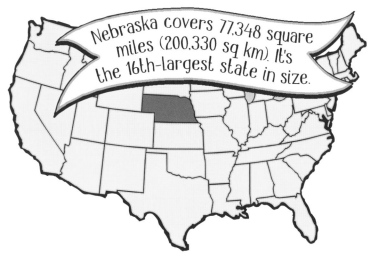

Nebraska covers 77,348 square miles (200,330 sq km). It's the 16th-largest state in size.

INDEX

A

Agate Fossil Beds, 7
animals, 4, 6, 7, 10, 11, 12, 13, 14, 15, 16, 27
Arbor Day, 34
Astaire, Fred, 26
Avoca, 12

B

Bayard, 8
Beatrice, 21
Bellevue, 19, 22, 28, 29
Bessey, Charles, 34, 35
botanists, 35
Brando, Marlon, 26
Bryan, William Jennings, 30
Buffalo Bill Rodeo, 26, 27
Burwell, 15

C

Cabela's, 33
Calamus State Fish Hatchery, 14, 15
California Trail, 20
Chadron, 18, 19
Chicken Flying Contest, 13
Chimney Rock, 8, 19
Clift, Montgomery, 26
climate, 9
Coburn, James, 26
Cody, William "Buffalo Bill," 26
cornhusking, 13
courts, 31
Czech festival, 23

D

Danish Day, 22
Dannebrog, 23
Dennis, Sandy, 26
Durham Museum, 25

E

elevation, 9

F

farming, 8, 11, 12, 13, 15, 17, 24, 32
Filley, 26
Fonda, Henry, 26
Ford, Gerald, 30
Fort Kearny, 21
Fort Lisa, 18
fossils, 6, 7
French exploration, 16
fur trade, 18, 19
Fur Trade Days, 19

G

Gering, 8
GermanFest, 23
Gothenburg, 20
governors, 31
Grand Island, 13, 24, 26
Grundlovsfest, 22, 23

H

Hall, Joyce C., 33
Hallmark Greeting Card Company, 33
Halsey, 34, 35
hand-planted forest, 34, 35
Hard Boiled Egg Eating Contest, 13
Harrison, 7
Hastings, 26
hatcheries, 14, 15
Homestead Act (1862), 20, 21
Homestead National Monument of America, 21

I

immigrants, 23
industries, 28, 32, 33

K

Kawasaki Motors Manufacturing, 32, 33
Kearney, 11

L

Laurel, 26
Lincoln, 6, 22, 30, 31, 32, 33, 34
Lisa, Manuel, 18

M

McGuire, Dorothy, 26
mining, 33
Missouri River, 8
Mitchell Pass, 9
Mormon Trail, 20
Morton, Julius Sterling, 34

N

National Cluck-Off, 12
national parks, 10
Native Americans, 16, 17
natural resources, 12, 15, 28, 33
Nebraska City, 34
Nebraska National Forest, 34, 35
Nebraska State Fair, 13, 27
Nebraskaland Days, 27
Niobrara River, 27
Nolte, Nick, 26
North Platte, 26, 27
North Platte River, 8

O

Offutt Air Force Base, 28, 29
Old Glory Blowout, 26
Omaha, 18, 22, 25, 26, 30
Omahas, 17
Oregon Trail, 18, 19, 20, 21

P

Pine Ridge, 9, 27, 34
pioneers, 8, 9, 19, 20
plants, 11, 20, 34, 35
Platte River, 8, 10, 11, 19, 22, 25, 27
population, 22
powwows, 16

R

raceways, 14
railroads, 24, 25

S

Sand Hills, 8, 35
sandhill cranes, 10, 11
Scott Lookout Tower, 35
Scotts Bluff, 8, 9, 19
settlers, 20, 21, 23
Sod House Museum, 20
South Platte River, 8
state capital, 31
state capitol, 31
state government, 31
state holidays, 34
state legislature, 31
state symbols, 10, 12, 30
statehood, 25
Strategic Air Command, 29
Stuhr Museum of the Prairie Pioneer, 24

T

Taylor, Robert, 26
transcontinental railroad, 24

U

U.S. Air Force, 29
U.S. Strategic Command, 28, 29
Union Pacific Railroad, 25
University of Nebraska, 34
University of Nebraska State Museum, 6

V

Viener Dog Race, 23

W

Winnebagos, 16, 17

Bye, Cornhusker State. We had a great time. We'll come back soon